It's made by one of the oldest manufacturers in the world. I bought it from a guy in George. And it's got a history attached to it. When I went back there in December he asked if he could buy it back from me. But I said no.

Kimberley is great for riding bicycles. It's flat around there. But it's nice to have hills. I ride a lot down near Mossel Bay. When I go on holiday I take a road bike as well as a mountain bike. I feel great when I go cycling. I just ride out on the road or ride around town or ride along next to the railway line. It's nice to be out in the open. Out in the *veld*. You can stop and watch a train go by.

I think this book is a very good thing. It's amazing that Stan and Nic had the guts to do something like this. And I think it's probably quite a sacrifice too. They're not going to become millionaires. It's really, how shall I say, a project from the heart.

Leonard Stanford
Corner-café/bicycle-repair-shop owner, and ex-velodrome rider

Bicycle Portraits

Leonard Stanford
Gladstone Avenue, De Beers, Kimberley, Northern Cape, South Africa
2010/08/06 18:04

'This is my town bicycle. If I am going somewhere safe, I use it. I have many bicycles I'm working on. I don't throw anything away. I am crazy about cycling, been cycling since I was 16. I used to do track riding – we had two tracks here in Kimberley, but now both are gone. So it's been years, but I want to ride track again before I die, one more time. I live alone, behind the workshop here, so when I get up in the morning I just walk through and I'm at work. I've always got something to do, I don't have a desire to go sit in the pub, drink and play pool and get up to nonsense – you know, those days are past. The old body also doesn't want to do it any more and there is no money, to be honest.'

Edward Paulus
Phillip Souden Street, Springbok, Northern Cape, South Africa
2011/04/11 09:06

'I used to have a BMX. Then I sold it, and I bought this bicycle from an old guy and built it up myself. I made this rack on the back here, and I raised my children on this rack – one is nine and the other almost two. I used to tie a crate onto the rack and that is where they used to sit. I took them shopping with me and they always came with me to the location. Poles, cement, firewood – I can bring anything home with this bicycle. I ride to Concordia, Okiep, Nababeep. I've even ridden to Pella with it – I left here in the morning at 6am and I got down there at 10am, and visited there for a while. On the way back I also left at 6am, but I only got back here at 11am – I had to rest a bit along the way. On the bike I had my clothes, food and water. I had my hat on my head for the sun. You see my back wheel? I've had to repair it with wire. The tyre has a tear, so I've wrapped wire around it to keep the tube from coming out. But I ride the bike!'

Stephanus Abelse
Corner Lower Main Road and Norfolk Road, Observatory, Cape Town, Western Cape, South Africa
2010/04/16 16:35

'I am on my way from the UCT Private Academic Hospital. I work with the maintenance team there. I'm headed home to Manenberg. It takes me almost an hour to get home every day, unless it's raining or too windy, then I take a taxi. But I'm used to my bike. It keeps me fresh and on the go. I've been cycling since I was 25 and I'm 60 now. But this is my daughter's bike. She got it from someone who said it came from Germany. It's still got the old white-wall tyres. But I don't want my daughter to ride – it's too dangerous. I can trust myself because I know how to brake and get out of the way of cars. The taxis are the dangerous ones. One day a taxi came up behind me. The driver wanted to stop here in front of me, but he couldn't wait and he nicked the handlebar. I looked at him and said, "Can't you see? I was in front of you and you swerved into me." He just swore at me. I put this mirror on. It was an old, broken motorbike mirror and I cut a new mirror myself: just sandpapered the edges, put some silicone on and put it in. I don't ride like this, looking over my shoulder. I rather keep my eye on the mirror.'

Mulna van Niekerk with Aldo and Zilke
Jacob Street, Boshof, Free State, South Africa
2011/02/28 15:58

Mulna: 'In the mornings I ride to work at my parents' petrol station,
I do the books, and then I go and fetch the kids. First I collect Zilke
from school and then I fetch Aldo. Zilke goes on the back and Aldo
in the front. Luckily it's all downhill to here. We have lunch at my
parents' and then we go home. This bike was a hand-me-down from
my brother. It's an old, old bike – a Bomber – but it's a good bike. It
doesn't have a lot of gears – just one and that's forward. It's all I need.
There's a guy here in town, *oom* Paul, who oils and fixes it for me.'
Zilke: 'My mom rides very well. She fetches us from school. After
school we go to see grandpa. And when we get home we have
to do our homework.'
Mulna: 'Sometimes we get pulled over by the traffic police and they
tell me that I'm overloaded! I just tell them not to worry because
I have heavy-duty tyres! But we stick to the back roads…'

Lynne Matthysen
Stasie Street, Stellenbosch, Western Cape, South Africa
2010/10/07 16:42

'The bike takes me to class faster than walking. I like to squeeze as much as I can into my day. You also don't have any problems with parking. When I first got it I realised that walking was a *schlep* for me, because it was just too slow, ha ha. This bike I bought about five and a half years ago. Its name is Florentine, because when I bought it there was a German exchange student who started walking with me to the shop, and his name was Florent or something. It stands outside as there is no space inside – that is why it looks like this! I've been living in Stellenbosch for seven years. It is a cute town, but it has its good and bad points. In general, though, I enjoy it here. It is close to the sea, the beach and the city. You can walk and cycle to most places. It is very calm. One thing I miss since I started cycling is that when you walk you have more time to see things, like trees. On the other hand when you cycle you also see different things from when you use a car or even when you walk. I've realised that other drivers and road users do not see cyclists, they only see cars. It has happened a few times where I followed the rules of the road, but then they almost caused an accident because they didn't see me. Although there are a few girls who cycle in Stellenbosch, not many cycle to class. Most people who use bicycles on campus are exchange students. When I've stayed late on campus I'd rather cycle home than walk. I made a basket for my bicycle because I couldn't find one at the two bike shops in town. Since then they got baskets, but by then I'd already made my own.'

Hlez Dube
Samuel Street, Lethabong, Tembisa, Gauteng, South Africa
2011/06/26 12:49

'I have just bought this bicycle from my boss. I enjoy cycling very much. What I like about this bicycle is that it is sporty, it's a racer. I don't cycle for a club; I just cycle on my own, for personal things, transport and local trips. Life in Tembisa is good for someone who knows what he wants. And as long as you have work and can afford the principal things in life, everything is fine. But if you don't have a job, everything can turn sour. *Ja*. The guys behind me here do sewing – that's how they earn a living. When people need some alterations or repairs they come here. At the moment I'm not permanently employed, but I'm a qualified plumber, I can do electricity, I can do tiling, most of the things in construction – bricklaying, plastering, paving and things like that.'

Marco Milford
Main Road, Port Nolloth, Northern Cape, South Africa
2011/04/11 12:03

'I cycle to get to town faster. We don't have money for things like cars, so bicycles are more affordable. We just cycle from the location to the town to do some shopping. Like now – I'm heading to the petrol pumps to buy some petrol. With the bicycle it is more comfortable for me to get back home. The petrol is for the ocean. We go out with these outboard motors to do fishing. We are going tomorrow, we already went today. The weather caused us to return early; the fish wouldn't bite. The boat belongs to an uncle I work with. *Snoek*, yellowtail – we are allowed to catch 60 per day. The fish needs to be 80 millimetres and bigger. This is not my bicycle; it is one that I'm hiring. You pay R1 per hour, so I just rent this bicycle from a guy so I can come to town and finish my things and so on. He has five bicycles. Many people hire them; some days I get there and the bicycle is already hired. It doesn't have brakes, but he will probably put them on sometime. I just brake by putting my foot on the back wheel.'

Malefetsane Qabalatsane
Moiloa Street, Phuthaditjhaba, Free State, South Africa
2011/03/09 10:36

'I live in Phamong, QwaQwa. I am on my way home. My problem
when I use the bicycle is that I have to walk up and down the hills
– I can only ride on flat surfaces, because I have a leg injury from
a car accident. Before I used this bicycle, I was a marathon runner.
I ran Comrades, Two Oceans … a lot of marathons. Now I use the
bicycle to train. I love it – okay, it's an old bicycle but it is important
to me because it keeps me fit and at the same time it's my legs.
I bought it when I was working at the mine in Klerksdorp. When
I lost my job I brought it back home. I load metals, zinc and scraps,
on the carrier at the back and sell them at the scrap yard. That's
why it is so big. It helps me – I get a few cents to live on.'

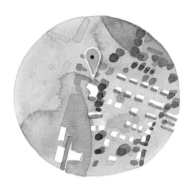

Khayalethu Dyantyi with Roven 'Worsie' Scheepers and Lutando Ikhonto
Cookhouse, Eastern Cape, South Africa
2010/12/16 16:13

'We're just riding around here, as far as the tar road. We're on school
holidays. My dad painted this bicycle so nicely. He doesn't mind if we
ride on his bicycle.'

Searchmore Kabatchi
Samuel Street, Lethabong, Tembisa, Gauteng, South Africa
2011/06/26 11:58

'Ah, my name is Searchmore. I took a ride to get some chips for my
kids and I'm on my way home now. My kids are still young, but I want
to teach them how to ride, just like me. Wherever I go I take my bike.
Even over long distances. I bought this bike from one of my bosses
– it's from Japan, it's got Japanese writing all over it. And it's strong
and light because it is made from aluminium. I'll keep it for my babies
for one day when they are grown up.'

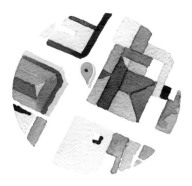

Peter Briggs
Long Street, Cape Town, Western Cape, South Africa
2010/04/14 17:10

'I've had this bike for about four months. I'm a minister in a church
and it was another minister who gave me the bike. I used to cycle
long ago, but stopped for about 20 years. Now I've started again
because I don't have a car, ha ha, and I have to get around. The
bike showed me how very unfit I am – and it gave me a chance to
remedy that. I am doing it bit by bit; I cycle a little further each time.
There are quite a few ministers who cycle and some of my colleagues
have even done the Cape Argus Pick n Pay Cycle Tour, but I wouldn't:
I cycle for transport, not for madness! In traffic I've never felt very
safe. I used to cycle in Pretoria, and even Cape Town's taxi drivers
are not as bad as Pretoria's ordinary drivers.'

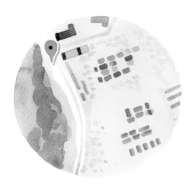

William Jaar
Rainbow City Street, Port Nolloth, Northern Cape, South Africa
2011/04/11 12:34

'I bought this bicycle from a guy who sells them. At least I got it for a good price. I'm a fisherman, you know, so I gave him some money and the rest I made up in fish – that was our deal. I like riding. I taught myself how to ride when I was young: first you fall a few times and then you start getting it right. Nowadays I'm so used to riding, I've completely forgotten that I ever fell! But the bike has to be right. I don't like to ride a bicycle without brakes, it's unsafe. I just ride around here, say, to the graveyard or to McDougalls Bay. Sometimes I put some music on, on my phone, and put my headphones on and just ride around listening to music, maybe Michael Jackson. But being a fisherman is tough. We struggle to catch enough fish. Port Nolloth is a difficult place … the wind howls one day and then it's fiery hot, that's how it goes. It's a back-to-front place.'

Tanki Mohapeloa
N8, near the South Africa/Lesotho border, Free State, South Africa
2011/03/04 13:52

'It's because of this bicycle that I am able to make money, so if you are going to give me some, I want it. I am a Mosotho and I hustle with this wagon. There are no jobs, so I have made this my job. I take tourists' luggage in it and it helps me to make a living. People come and ask me to carry their cargo to certain destinations and then give me money. Anything that a car carries, I can carry with this. I can carry a cement bag. I can carry a bed … from Lesotho to South Africa. When I work hard, of course I sweat a lot. It's not an easy thing to do.'

Claudette van der Walt
Church Street, Adelaide, Eastern Cape, South Africa
2010/12/16 11:46

'I cycle because it is not easy for me to walk. Quite a few years ago I was in an accident that resulted in brain injury. Since then I walk with difficulty. The people at my school realised that I would find it easier to cycle, so they designed this bicycle for me and came up with the name *Vinnige Fanie.* It's a special school for people who find it difficult to get on with life. It is designed so that there is only one level, so everyone can get to class quickly and on time. The teachers there were very understanding and physiotherapy was part of the classes. I'm now finished with school, though. I've had *Vinnige Fanie* since Standard 6. I'm now … ha ha, don't get a fright … 42! I'm good friends with this bicycle.'

Isac 'Biopace' Cossa
Kwame Nkrumah Avenue, Maputo, Mozambique
2011/07/05 09:57

'My bicycle club name is "Biopace". This name was initiated here
at the club and went on to gain fame. In my daily life I wake up in
the morning and go to school with my Alpina, which has Biopace
chainrings. After school I go home, check out what I can eat, then
I come here to the club to learn maintenance skills and how to clean
my bicycle, and lots more about it. The person who welcomed me
here at the club is Betinho. He is my mentor. My routine is that! School,
bicycle club and then home. It's more or less that! I got my bicycle
from my older brother. I asked him for it and he gave it to me. I like
this bicycle – with love – its name is Alpina and it's exact, exact,
exactly that!'

Johan Schade
Coronation Road, Maitland, Cape Town, Western Cape, South Africa
2010/01/12 18:12

'I'm on my way home from Bellville to Milnerton. I've been riding
bikes since I was four – BMXs and stuff. It's only recently that I've
been riding longer distances. I ride to work about three times a week,
depending on the weather. Other times I take the motorbike or car.
The bike was a hand-me-down through three families – inherited and
passed on and fixed up – a real *kanniedood*. I had an expensive
bike as well but I wrote it off. That's what happens when you try to
do BMX tricks on a mountain bike. This bike is a bit customised:
it's been coming along for 13 or 14 years. It's been through off-road
riding, it's been ramped, my friend even towed me with a motorbike.
I held his hand and he pulled me along the N1 highway. The fastest
he said we were going was 140 kilometres per hour – then the front
bearing seized up and the wheel locked. I went over the bars. I've
broken everything – legs, arms, hurt my back. Been to the ICU.
Been all over.'

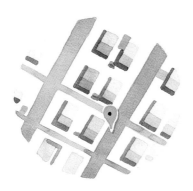

Remo Baker
Rosebud Street, KwaNokuthula, Riversdale, Western Cape, South Africa
2010/04/25 18:33

'Why do I cycle? Because it's fun! Also it's exercise and, I mean, there is lots you can do with it. I've been cycling for about five years now. I bought this bicycle and I've modified it a little, putting in extra pipes and different tyres. It means everything to me.'

Esau Ngwenya
Eeufees Street, Bethal, Mpumalanga, South Africa
2011/07/10 17:46

'My older brother gave me this bicycle about three years ago after someone stole my old black *dikwiel*. He had this bicycle for many, many years. He's 54 now. I like these old *dikwiel* bicycles – they last, not like these racers that break so easily. After they stole my old bicycle I started locking it here outside this hairdresser every day while I'm at work. I didn't ask them to watch it, but I know that they can see it out of their window and no thieves will try and steal it. I leave my home at 6am and cycle here, where they fetch me at 6.30am to take me to the farm where I work in the workshop. I get dropped here again in the evening. I was born here in Bethal 42 years ago. I have two sons and two daughters – all still at school. At the moment I'm fixing up my house, but I hope to buy a car one day. Then I will pass this bicycle on to my eldest son. My wife can ride a bit, but she is scared!'

Jo Rawson
Government Avenue, Company Gardens, Cape Town, Western Cape, South Africa
2010/08/27 19:38

'I cycle because I love it and find it very liberating. It's a good way to
see the city and it's so convenient. It is also much quicker to ride than
to sit in a car, and it's a good way to interact with people. Everyone
has been so friendly. I only got this bike yesterday, ha ha. I look like
I'm an expert, hey? I had a mountain bike, but I've always wanted a
city bike. I wanted one with a basket in the front and a little clip thing
at the back so I can carry my stuff. It's a belated birthday present from
my fiancé. It has a Peugeot frame from France. He looked and looked
for one, and it arrived about three months late. He is big into cycling:
our little 63-square metre flat has four bikes in it ... and one in the
storeroom! I rode it all day and I'm just on my way back from yoga.
It is somehow so much safer than walking, because you are moving
a bit faster. The bike is very liberating and agile – those are probably
the two words it makes me think about.'

Ronnie Godfrey with his son, Marshall
Luxolweni, Hofmeyr, Eastern Cape, South Africa
2010/12/13 16:29

Ronnie: 'We have just come from my father's farm in Southfield.
Last week we went there because I was sick and I couldn't look
after myself. My dad got this bicycle as a Christmas present about
five years ago and he lent it to me today. Marshall rides here in front
of me, so I can make sure his legs don't get in the way of the wheels.
And we put the pillow here, so he won't get tired. He has a bicycle
too – a little yellow one.'
Marshall: 'I can ride but my bicycle wheel is flat at the moment
… my dad shaved my hair, it's cool, hey?'

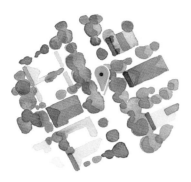

Charl Oettle
Meiring Street, Paglande, Worcester, Western Cape, South Africa
2011/05/07 09:43

'Cycling is by far the most rational way of riding around Worcester, which is flat. If there is a busy road you can just go one block up and you miss all the "busy-ness". I live very close to work, but by having the bicycle I can duck out to town in a break and it gives me another 10 minutes for my coffee in the morning! I've got a *bakkie* because a car is sometimes needed to fill in the gaps. But for day-to-day life here I can do 90%-plus by bicycle. It is an intensely practical tool for me. Not with terribly much romance, it is just a very functional and clear way of running one's life. There are very few weather constraints in Worcester – it doesn't rain much and you're not too exposed to the wind. My daily commuting bike has a handmade Francois du Toit frame and has a lovely liveliness to it. When the fellow wanted only R2 000 for it I thought it was a pity to leave it. I also have this touring bike, which was handmade in England according to my brother's specifications. He upgraded his and gave me this one, which rides like a dream, and has an old Brooks saddle and panniers, so when I do need to carry heavier stuff then

I can do so. This number on the top tube is the number of a zeppelin – my brother is very keen on zeppelins. He has ridden to work for years and years in Johannesburg, he is also a doctor. I worked in Holland years ago and bought a bike – an old, tatty, second-hand back-pedal-brake affair. That society is geared to cyclists: they think about cyclists and know about them, and take them into account.'

Johannes Diko
Bird Street, Kayamandi, Stellenbosch, Western Cape, South Africa
2010/09/29 17:35

'The thing is, cycling is good exercise. You know, I like it and I cycle
to work. I feel that I'm safe – safer than if I take the train. I've been
cycling for four years now. They've bumped me before near the golf
course … but it wasn't the end, I kept on cycling. I often get a flat
tyre, but I fix it there and then. I've had these flags since the World
Cup. Now people can see me better and the cars keep a bit more
of a distance from me. This *vuvuzela* is for when I'm on a road, passing
entrances. If, for example, a car is coming out, I blow it so that they
know I'm coming. Only the front brakes work here. The whip, ha ha,
it is just for safety on the road, in case someone wants to attack me
– you never know when you might get attacked. I've not used it so
far though, ha ha. Look, cycling saves me money – that is the main
reason I cycle.'

Tumi Tholwana
Hoog Street, Thaba Nchu, Free State, South Africa
2011/03/03 16:44

'I use this bicycle as a means of transport, and for fun and exercise.
It is modified with extra handlebars here at the back so that I can
carry another person if they need a ride. I've only had it for about
four weeks; someone from a nearby village gave it to me. I like to
play ball, and I use the bike to go and play in villages that are far
away. The face paint, ha ha, it actually means "I'm ugly on charts"
– I was going to show off in a soccer match. I play number 5, a
defender. I'm not scared to live and play next to this place, even
though there are coffins here…'

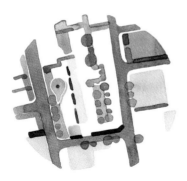

Albert van der Watt
Somerset Road, De Waterkant, Cape Town, Western Cape, South Africa
2010/04/13 14:40

'I enjoy riding bikes, it's an easy way to get around and you have
no parking problems. And it's quick to get in and out of the traffic.
It's convenient, you know – save the car, leave it at home and get fit.
I've got a car and a *bakkie* at home, and I've got this bike and
a mountain bike. I live in Table View – I've just come here to this
cellphone shop and then I'm going to go back to my auto-electrical
workshop in town. I've had some close calls on the bike, you know,
once or twice with those container trucks on West Coast Road.
But other than that I haven't really had anything happen … but
I have fallen hard, ha ha! And I wouldn't say I feel safe on the road.
Especially with these trucks. It's mainly the trucks that I worry about
– the cars aren't so bad. You always have close calls with the trucks.
I suppose they can't move over very far. I see the people are busy
making a cycling lane for us now, from Table View to town. I can't
wait for that to be finished. It'll be nice in the mornings – just get in
that lane and go. Hopefully soon…'

Thinus Opperman
Martini Henry Avenue, Elandspoort, Gauteng, South Africa
2011/06/25 12:57

'I ride from here to the city, to Daspoort, to Pretoria Gardens … and come back through the tunnel that goes under the mountain. It took them about five or six years to dig it and now they've rebuilt it so cars and people can go through. But it's very muddy in there, a big mess. Maybe I'll go to Pretoria North, or to the shops to buy whatever I need. Sometimes I'll go for a walk in the *veld* just to see what's going on, and maybe I'll find something – a plant or something like that – and I'll dig it up and plant it here at home in a little pot. I got this bicycle as a gift from a friend. I had some tubes and tyres fitted; it cost me a few rands. I also got new cables and pedals. It cost me about R550 for the whole story. I sprayed it yellow, but it still needs some white spray, a second coat for the front here.'

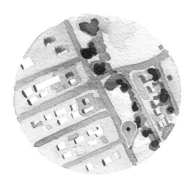

Given Mabuza with his father, Mandla
Mahube Valley, Mamelodi East, Pretoria, Gauteng, South Africa
2010/04/11 12:25

'I like the bicycle to go to school. I like the bicycle to check my friends.
I like the bicycle to go to the shop, and I can use it for racing.'

Thulani Papa
Langa, Cape Town, Western Cape, South Africa
2010/01/14 17:10

'I fix TVs, DVDs and all that stuff, and I use this bicycle to go and get parts. I got it from an old Indian man, Lucky Govender, my friend. He knows how to repair bicycles and he's a technician as well. You see, I had another bicycle once and one day I got a puncture. I left it at his place to fix, but when I went to fetch it he told me it had been stolen. He gave me his bike, this red bicycle, to replace it. It was a racing bike, but I took the drop handlebars off and I put on these tall handlebars. It has speed, it runs very well and it's very light. People around here don't want to ride it because it doesn't look like a normal bike. I also put on only a front brake, and I've made it really strong, so that if someone rides too fast and they touch the brake they will fall down. Whenever people borrow it they come back to me and they say, "This bike took me down!" Sometimes the person brings it back and the handles are skew, and I can see he did fall. I don't ask what happened, because I know the story!'

My first bike was cerise, with white balloon tyres. On the side was written 'Convertible'. This meant, I thought, the bike could fold like my brother's friend Louis's green one, but I could never work out how mine collapsed. It had 'fairy' wheels (or 'ferry' wheels, I never worked that out either), which my dad eventually removed.

My older brother had a brown BSA, with beautiful cast braze-ons for a pump, drop bars turned upwards and stripped of tape, running only a back brake. I remember him practising 'broadies' in the garden. On his return from the local motocross track one Sunday, the bike was plastered in yellow and black 'Bardahl' stickers. Later, I was given that bike as a birthday present. My father had Johnson Cycle Works touch it up, fit a front brake and replace the drops with straight bars. I feel ashamed now when I recall the disappointment I felt: the bike seemed neutered.

But it did mean transport and a measure of freedom, and I started riding to school with my older sister. Unfortunately, my mother's insistence that I stay on the pavements was limiting. I felt sure that, at a similar age, both my siblings had been allowed on the tarmac. This really bit when my brother cycled from Johannesburg to Durban with a group of friends, on the hard shoulder of the national road.

I was eventually allowed on the road, and when I outgrew my brown bike I got a bronze 12-speed Western Flyer Monza. My friend Alastair had one similar; together we covered vast distances. His fork-mounted odometer once clocked more than 100 kilometres in one day. I recall cold Highveld mornings, the two of us in matching Adidas windbreakers as we rode to Sunday school. Later there was a brief dalliance with a BMX which I rode into the ground, eventually selling it for R40.

When my father gave up smoking, he bought himself a sluggish Puma mountain bike with bullhorn handlebars, sponge grips and a big, soft seat. When he lost interest, I took it to university in Pietermaritzburg, where it served as transport, but never earned much affection. Later, I bought a bike for R200 from a friend: a blue Nishiki, with cantilever brakes and more gears than I ever used. Although the thought of mountain biking appalled me, I often found myself up in the forests, where riders would soon build trails. I eventually sold it to my girlfriend's brother for R100.

After university I followed my girlfriend to Cape Town, where I met artist Brett Murray, who became a sort of mentor. When I enquired about the old *dikwiel* bike in his studio, he directed me to Noor, who ran Progress Cycles from the Loop Street Mosque where he was caretaker. For R200, Noor fitted an old frame with riser bars and a rear brake I'd chosen, and I added a wire basket.

This bike soon cross-pollinated with my old mountain bike (which I bought back for R50). I eventually gave this away and rescued an old BMX from a friend's back yard. I restored it with all the parts I had desired as a child: Dia-Compe brakes, Suntour Beartrap pedals, Ukai rims. Although it made me smile, this bike was too small and I was too old, so I tried to cobble together a 26-inch BMX cruiser and found myself building a single-speed mountain bike. This was not as simple as I thought, and I sought advice from the inimitable Sheldon Brown, a curmudgeon from a bike shop outside Boston, Massachusetts.

Sheldon had a fleet of fixed-gears and was a repository of arcane information. His various websites detailed everything from his hat collection to a penchant for amateur musicals. From him I bought a simple chain-tension device, which was essential on most frames then. I even convinced a local cycling magazine to run an article I wrote on converting a mountain bike to single-speed. They included this in the oddball column at the end. Dedicated single-speed parts were scarce, and expensive when you found them, so I began designing and producing my own chainrings and sprockets.

My fleet soon doubled to include a commuter and, with encouragement from a former bike courier in London, I converted this to a fixed-gear. By then I was commuting every day and a simple, low-maintenance drivetrain made sense. I liked the way this set me apart, but at the heart of it lay my distaste for excessive parts and unnecessary expense. Besides, there were no real hills between home and work. My desire for simplicity had turned out to be complicated and, I guess, my taste for freedom unearthed some constraints. Trade-offs are inevitable, and what was once innocent and exciting manifests as something more complex in an adult.

It's gruelling out there amid motorists who are ignorant and contemptuous of the law. Cyclists don't do themselves any favours either. This was brought home when I biked in New York last year, enjoying the 1 100 kilometres of dedicated cycle lanes in a city filled with the whirr and click of bikes, where parking can be scarce among sidewalk racks and lampposts bristling with steel, rubber and aluminium.

This year I visited Portland, Oregon – arguably North America's cycling capital despite its persistently inclement weather. There I seldom ventured onto roads without bike lanes or that weren't bike boulevards, compelling motorists to give way at rush hour. San Francisco too, I saw, is awash with bicycles. In all these cities, buses and trains mesh efficiently with all modes of non-motorised transport.

Cycling lost its innocence for me in another way, too, last year. In summer I regularly ride home across the lower slopes of Table Mountain; a safer option, I figure, than the mean streets of Woodstock. On a warm evening in December, as I began a long, slow climb, a black-clad figure stepped into the road and, crouched low, ran at me. I realised he was out to rob me, and in a flash decided to ride him down. It was only then that I noticed the knife in his hand. I yelled as we clashed. When I next looked up, I was some distance from my bike, while my assailant hovered menacingly. After a curiously civil conversation, he took my bag and fled.

The violence was certainly traumatic, but confusing and disturbing was that I understood my assailant's point of view. Such is the nature of South Africa that it's common for cyclists to navigate their R20 000 machines past people with nowhere to sleep, or who have fled war in their countries. This can't justify the violence, but it hints at a complex situation. This plays itself out in our relationship to bicycles too. We aren't a country like China or Malawi where the bicycle is a primary means of transport. Nor are we a developed country, like the US, where increasing numbers choose a bicycle. Most of our population probably aspire to drive a car and wouldn't be seen dead on a bike, while many cyclists own a car and only ride for recreation.

But this trend is shifting, and exceptions, more than proving it, are beginning to change the rule. Critical Mass rides are growing in several urban centres and no inner-city apartment is complete without a fixed-gear on the wall or a commuter in the stairwell. Much of this is a function of fashion and perhaps a burgeoning environmental awareness, but these influences trickle down to the wider population, and the presence of bicycles in a sustainable future is as tangible as the smell of fresh rubber filling any bike shop worth its salt.

Paul Edmunds
Artist, and enthusiastic and dedicated commuter and mountain biker

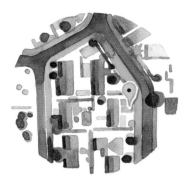

Pieter Engelbrecht
Williams Avenue, Newtown, Wellington, Western Cape, South Africa
2011/06/05 15:29

'I am Pieter Engelbrecht. I was born in Cape Town – that was a really really rough place. The places that you live in aren't rough, it's the people that live there that make it rough. I'm not originally from Wellington, I came here when I was already grown up. You know, I was a *sakkeroller*, a pickpocket – now that was my organisation. I used to be a rough guy. I decided that my sport should be cycling. I've never played rugby – I watch rugby, but I've never played it. I can't let 15 guys chase me around if I didn't do anything wrong, and at the end when they catch me they hurt me and then it's hospital time. So I decided cycling is my sport, and the talent I received is music – I'm a musician, into music. I enjoy riding around on my bike. And that is not to say that I only ride to the café and to the toilet – I hit the road to Worcester, Ceres, Hamlet, Porterville... Many know me because of my sport here in Wellington. And there are many who know me because of my talent here in Wellington. So I almost want to to say that I am famous for my sport and my talent here in Wellington. I am Pieter Engelbrecht, and those who have not yet heard of me will now hear of me! The club I ride with is from Paarl, the Yorkshire Wheelers, and I've been riding with them since 1980. I find it a real pleasure. This bicycle here is my dependable one. I have two more bicycles, but this is the one I choose when I decide I want to ride to Ceres or Worcester or Hamlet – this I the one I depend on. I take the tools I need but I don't have to worry that it will break here and break there. I'm very happy with this bicycle of mine. I would never trade it for any modern bicycle. I love it because it might look simple, but it has Shimano 105 components. You get other parts like Dura-Ace and Suntour and that, but 105 for me is the best. You have to look after a bicycle like this, you can't afford to get this bike stolen – a thief might sell a bike like this for a shameful R100...'

Kevin Gannon
Main Road, Woodstock, Cape Town, Western Cape, South Africa
2011/01/06 19:55

'I'm on my way back from work. I cycle to and from work every day.
I'm here on contract for a few years. When I came, since that's the
way I got around at home in the US, I decided to cycle here, although
people said it was not very commuter-friendly. But I haven't really had
any problems. I cycle from Observatory to where Parliament is in the
city. I'm an architect and work for an international NGO; we are doing
projects all over Africa, but we are headquartered in Cape Town. So
when I'm not riding my bike I'm usually on a plane flying around the
continent. I love riding to work, and if I couldn't, I'd get really frustrated
and stressed. I lived in New York City 20 years ago. Everybody said
it was dangerous to cycle in Cape Town and I said, "Well, can it be
any worse than New York City 20 years ago?" I found it hasn't been.
I have more fun riding in urban traffic than I do on a long tour through
the countryside. It's just more interactive – like a video game with taxis
and buses. A month ago I busted my collarbone. I slammed on the
brakes and went over the handlebars. So now I've got a 10 centimetre
strip of metal and 10 screws in my collarbone. But it's fine, sort of…'

Thabang Ditlhareng
Bultfontein Road, Kimberley, Northern Cape, South Africa
2010/08/05 15:29

'To go to school, that is what I use this bicycle for. It is a bit far to walk – I won't be able to be there on time. We are heading home now. It helps you to exercise your legs. I have a bigger bicycle at home. I was just testing this one today. The bicycle helps me to get wherever I want to go.'

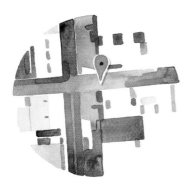

Shruthi Nair
Fox Street, Maboneng Precinct, Johannesburg, Gauteng, South Africa
2011/05/28 17:43

'We decided to get bikes a few months ago, because in winter
you need some form of exercise and to get outside. We've lived in
countries where there is a biking culture, so we thought we'd try and
do that in Jo'burg. I've never driven and don't have a licence, so it is
a good way for me to get from A to B. It is scary, you have to be alert,
but it is probably the best way to explore the city. I was born in India.
When I was three we moved to Holland. I've also lived in Korea.
But *ja*, Jo'burg, which is such a beautiful city, is starting to become
regenerated. My boss built these bike stands and wants to encourage
people who live in this building to buy bikes and cycle around in
a "bike gang". It is one thing riding around by yourself, but if there
are two, three, four people, it's an experience. It is a great way to
bond with other people, you learn about the city – it's like going
on a treasure hunt. Both my parents are environmental and social
activists, so I started engaging with the local crèches and we set
up a foundation to help them.'

Qibintulo Xhosa
Qomoyi Street, Nonzwakazi, De Aar, Northern Cape, South Africa
2010/07/30 13:45

'I just cycle to work and back, twice a week. I don't walk because it is far. My legs aren't that great for walking – I'm an old man. The bicycle doesn't break down much, but I had to replace the back rim and cog. It cost R300. My son used to ride his own bicycle, but it was stolen, so now he borrows mine when my wife sends him to fetch things. There is no work around here at the moment. The people are struggling.'

Asher Tafara
Sir Lowry Road, Woodstock, Cape Town, Western Cape, South Africa
2010/11/05 12:42

'The bike helps me do the work of selling medicines, you see. I travel with the bike to get herbs and medicines on the mountains. I do healing of the people and sell medicines for a living. I'm heading to the mountains now. I look for any kind of special herbs, you know, for drinking – the usual stuff. I've been cycling for about three years and I enjoy it for sure. I like it for keeping fit too.'

John Jacobs
Blanco Boulevard, Kingswood Golf Estate, George, Western Cape, South Africa
2010/12/26 17:32

'My mom and dad had 21 children, but some are dead. Two of them drank paraffin, some got diseases and others were murdered. There are only about nine left. We all split up because my parents didn't have much money. From 1974 until 1987 I was in 14 different jails. Big jails – I was a troublesome guy. But now I'm really rehabilitated, for the rest of my life. On Tuesday I got a house from the government. I'm trying to make it beautiful and neat as quickly as possible so that I can get the people back who I lost when I spent that time in jail. I've been riding for 12 years and I enjoy it. This is my 10th bicycle. Every winter I have to pawn my bicycle at the pawn shop because I don't have work, then when I get money again I go fetch my bike. But sometimes it's gone and then I have to get another one. I am on my way from Fancourt now. I'm a golf caddie there. I enjoy carrying at the golf course, but there are some problems these days – people are starting to use golf carts.'

Kurt Abrahams
Bergzich Avenue, Genadendal, Western Cape, South Africa
2010/07/24 16:51

'I built this bike from scratch, man. Started with just the yellow frame.
Got a pair of wheels from a friend and then oiled it up. The gears
don't work. That is how I go. Sprayed it red. Cycling is an easier
way of transport, there's less pollution and it's more convenient.
Where I go, the bicycle goes – to work, to the shops, to friends
and to my girlfriend. It is my main source of transport. I think it's
good to use the bicycle, especially in a town like this. Lots of people
are eager to ride bicycles here. To me the bicycle means destiny,
because I reach my destiny.'

Wilma Plaatjies and **Rico Syster**
R43, Jonkersrivier farm, Western Cape, South Africa
2011/05/07 15:03

Wilma: 'My name is Wilma, I'm 12 years old, I live on Jonkersrivier
and we really enjoy riding the bicycle. We don't have strong tyres
and we don't have things to pedal on.'
Rico: 'My name is Rico, I'm six years old, me and Wilma are cousins.
My mother works in the vineyards. The mountains are beautiful here.'
Wilma: 'We sit here on this saddle that is broken. We step on the
ground with our feet and then the bicycle goes. When we go uphill
we push it, and when we go downhill we ride on it. We haven't had
it for very long.'
Rico: 'Uncle Vellie has a bicycle.'
Wilma: 'We go to school by bus.'

Martin Goosen
Van der Merwe Street, De Aar, Northern Cape, South Africa
2010/07/30 12:25

'Cycling is fun and it is healthy, my brother. The doctor told me I need to cycle and walk as much as I can – I have heart problems. It saves money and what is healthier than cycling? I worked for 43 years for the railways and I cycled for those 43 years. I was a driver, and I cycled day and night, winter and summer. I feel very healthy and I love it. That is why I keep cycling – I'd rather cycle than drive in the car, especially here in town. On Sunday afternoons I cycle far, around the town or to the railways, and visit people along the way. I feel very happy and proud of my bicycle. I love it so much.'

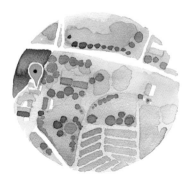

Polani Nontyi
Russell Park farm store, R400, Eastern Cape, South Africa
2010/12/18 08:51

'I love this bicycle, because I can use it for everything – to go to the shops and to school, from Monday to Friday. When I go to the shops I can load some things onto it and when I go to school I can load my books onto it. I want my grandfather to buy me a new tyre so I can fix it.'

Peter Abrahams
Kloof Street, Gardens, Cape Town, Western Cape, South Africa
2011/04/18 15:14

'People don't cycle because there is no cycling culture outside the sport of cycling. I don't do it for fitness; I do it because I feel it makes more sense. And also because I stay in the city centre and it is easy for me to get to places. You must not forget how apartheid has caused people to, like, live in places outside the city centre. You know, in times gone by, my parents lived in District Six and we got moved through forced removals to a place called Fairways, which is out in Wynberg. Now yes, you can cycle to your school, but many people are afraid because there aren't any proper cycling lanes. Also the distances between places are big. If you stay in areas where everything is more self-sufficient, where you have all the amenities, shops and things like that, then you can use a bicycle. People think cycling is expensive, but it's not true. You can buy a second-hand bike like I did for, like, R600. Then it could also be seen as dangerous. Cycling on the roads is more dangerous than mountain biking – the motorists don't have respect for cyclists. I had a BMX when I was a teenager and I loved it. I went to Amsterdam years ago. It was 2001 or 2002 – no, when was the Twin Towers? It was that year that I first encountered cycling in city centres and in Amsterdam. I said, I'm going to cycle when I return home. I came back and got myself a terrible mountain bike. I didn't care; the thing is, I got a cheap bike because I'm afraid of theft. I stayed in Vredehoek on the third floor and you know, taking the bicycle down, I had to be Superman. I loved it. I don't really like using my car at all. Yes, at night I have to use it to get to work and socialise and things like that. But I prefer my bicycle. I always have my backpack on; it is an easy way to get groceries. My wife is like, "Why do you come home with only one loaf of bread?" But I can actually get, like, R300's worth of groceries in my backpack. At the moment, I'm a DJ in transition. I've played professionally since I was 21 … I'm 35 now. I'm a contributor on Heart Radio on a show called Beatbox every Saturday. I'm also an aspiring producer and I'm pursuing a career of life coaching, actually – a programme called *Time To Think*.'

Vernon Versveld
Black River Parkway, Maitland, Cape Town, Western Cape, South Africa
2010/09/13 16:33

'I ride my bicycle because it is the cheapest way of transport. If
I didn't ride, it would cost me R250 a month. A bike like this costs
about R1 000, so after you've been riding for four months you've
paid for your bike. But you always should have money for tyres,
wheels, or for something that goes wrong. Good advice for any cyclist
is to have a spare bicycle hanging in your garage. If you don't have
a spare bicycle, keep a spare front wheel, put a tyre and tube on it,
and have a spare back wheel. I've been cycling a long time – easily
about 20 years. I cycle on this road every day. It is not dangerous.
I would say the bicycle is really my whole life, because wherever I go,
I go on the bicycle. If I go shopping, I hang it on my handlebars. I even
have a small trailer that I hook onto the bike if I want to carry a bag
of cement or whatever. I actually do woodwork, but there is nothing
at the moment. There is no work now – everything is dead and quiet.'

Innocent Manjo
Sir Lowry Road, Woodstock, Cape Town, Western Cape, South Africa
2011/01/26 13:44

'My name is Innocent. I'm a cycle rider. I was born in Zimbabwe
in 1988 and grew up in an orphanage, and I was adopted in South
Africa. My life is not complete. I don't know who I really am. It's like
I'm in three pieces, my heart is in three pieces, my life is in three
pieces – like this bicycle when I found it.'

Thomas Richardmagou
S558, outside Orania, Free State, South Africa
2010/08/01 17:15

'I go to work with the bicycle every morning at 7am. It's good to loosen up my legs and let my blood circulate in the mornings, so as you see me here I'm in good condition! The people at work gave me this bicycle. I only need to patch the tyres. The thing that worries me are these pedals, I'm scared they'll hurt me when I'm drunk. I'm scared of the bicycle; I don't cycle when I'm drunk. I'm not sure how often, because when I have some money, we drink on weekends. The bicycle's name is Blackstone.'

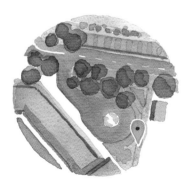

John North
University of Pretoria, Hillcrest, Pretoria, Gauteng, South Africa
2010/04/08 08:50

'My wife and I lived in Ireland for three years. Shortly before we came
back to South Africa, we decided we wanted to tour around Europe.
We took the car from Dublin, using the ferry, travelled to England
and bought two folding Bromptons in Oxford. We travelled to the
Netherlands, through Europe and down to Rome. We used the bikes
for sightseeing whenever we stopped. Since I've been back in South
Africa I've been using this bike to get to work. I feel there are far too
many cars on the road, and people are intolerant towards cyclists.
I'm determined not to be one of the angry single-occupant vehicles
on Pretoria's streets.'

Sithembiso 'Smarty' Petros
R335, outside Addo, Eastern Cape, South Africa
2010/12/19 09:30

'They call me "Smarty" because my father used to work for a company
called Smarty and they used to give me clothes. I got this bicycle from
my father's boss. It was a surprise to me because I'm not working – he
just gave it to me. He gave everyone who works there a bicycle and
then he also gave me one, because there are maybe nine workers
and there were 17 bicycles. I've had it only a week! *Yoh*, I like it so
much, *yoh*, *yoh*, *yoh*… Every day I'm on the road. I'm on my way
to the café; they sent me there to buy meat. Before this one I had
another bicycle, but it was small, smaller than this one, and it got
broken. I'm 18 now, but I didn't finish school; I stopped in 2008.
I was supposed to finish this year, but I didn't have money. Next
year I will be attending night school.'

Britney Koopman with her brother, Alamandro
Barkly Road, Homestead, Kimberley, Northern Cape, South Africa
2010/08/05 18:14

'I just ride around here and to the shops. I don't cycle to school
because it is too dangerous for me. I always cycle with my brother.
I've been cycling since 2008. My favourite thing is just to ride around,
and I like it because it gives me energy.'

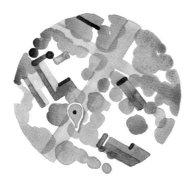

Gabriel Moloi
Oxford Street, Rosebank, Johannesburg, Gauteng, South Africa
2010/06/05 17:32

'I cycle almost every day because this is my transport. At first it was just a simple bike and then I made it to look like this myself. I like my job. I'm a security guard by profession. I like cycling, but I'm going to get a better bicycle, you see. I don't have materials, so this is just a frame of what I can do. This is just an idea. It has music, it has lights, it has indicators – it looks like a police bike. This light comes on and this one comes on as well, so it looks nice at night and I'll be visible anywhere where I go. I cycle almost 25 kilometres one way. I work at Absa Bank in Rivonia. I can go very far – this bike is like a car. The hooter has different sounds. This is a radio, I listen to 94.7.'

Salmon Mojaki
Lang Street, Campbell, Northern Cape, South Africa
2010/08/10 17:37

'Well, I started cycling when I was a little guy. I've always been keen on cycling as I realised it is something that will help me out. I can travel far. It is the best transport I've had. This is an old frame, but it is one of the strongest frames you get. I've just put on some new parts. Currently I'm not working, but most of the time I go to visit my brother on the farms. I live here with my mom and dad. My dad and mom used to cycle. My dad's Trek was a 12-52, that was the best: that is a 12-tooth cog at the back wheel and a 52-tooth gear at the front. The bicycle means a lot to me, it is as good as my whole life, ha ha. I'll never get rid of it, I'll keep it until my child can use it.'

Robert Swartz
9th Street, Homevale, Kimberley, Northern Cape, South Africa
2010/08/05 17:06

'I rode for the council all the years I was working. I was a postman,
then later, with a motorbike, I collected parcels at the airport and
the station. I worked for the council for 42 years. I used to earn one
pound seven shillings a week. That is like R10,75. Yes, a week! Ha
ha. Now I get R2 800 pension. I was born here and went to school
here. I bought this bike here in Kimberley. It's pleasurable. It keeps
me healthy. I can't complain about pain, nothing. I don't drink, I don't
smoke. My hobby is riding. I ride everywhere – I don't care how far
it is. Me and my brothers and sisters used to play cricket, soccer,
rugby and netball, and swim. We were always making jokes, ha ha,
always being happy. It's not the colour of your skin that matters. God
is always there. Go to church, teach the children to play sports, keep
yourself clean inside and outside. Smile and the whole world will smile
with you. I love God, he keeps me on my way. I guess I'm getting older
now, but I'm still on my bicycle – winter, summer. I feel good. I'm still fit.'

Johannes van Wyk with Chris, Danisha and Sarie
Pickering Avenue, Lindene, Kimberley, Northern Cape, South Africa
2010/08/08 13:40

'At our home we fix bicycles and our dad always used to ride, and so
we also made it a part of us. We understand all the problems of bikes,
buckled wheels and all those things, and we fix them. We use them all
the time, we ride everywhere, out to Boshoff Road, about 60 kilometres
away, to soccer, to work … everywhere. My first frame broke so I've
built this frame up, with speakers, amp and a cellphone. There are
many people here in Kimberley who have speakers on their bikes.
For me and my family, the bicycle is just like a car. We are on our
way to Green Point now, we're going to visit there and we'll come
back later.'

Amos Mphuti
Komane Street, Qalabotjha, Villiers, Free State, South Africa
2010/04/05 12:55

'I've ridden everywhere with this bike, even as far as Harrismith,
Frankfort, Tweeling and Reitz. I've been riding it since 1967, it's an
old bicycle. Old! I've got carriers for the front and back. I've taken
off the front one, but if I have a load, I put it on. I hope my children
will also get into cycling so that they can go to new places.'

George Diba
R369, Hopetown, Northern Cape, South Africa
2010/08/03 17:26

'I ride to work in the mornings. I've had this one for over 20 years
now. I had others before but I kept this one. It has a light, but it needs
a bulb. I like cycling; I'm actually very proud of my bicycle. I cycle all
the time. Loaded on this bicycle is my car's battery and my food bag.
My car is at home. I only drive it a little, maybe on weekends. In the
week I only ride the bicycle. My wife cycles as well. She also works
in town, but she doesn't cycle to work. It is going okay here for us
in this town – we are used to it.'

David Mufamadi
Charles Street, Brooklyn, Pretoria, Gauteng, South Africa
2010/04/16 17:35

'My bike is good for me – if I want to get somewhere, I can be there on time, without using a taxi. This bike was a present after my last one was stolen. This one is okay, but the old one was my baby. I've been in Arcadia today to visit a friend, and we went to see some chicks, ha ha … you know they drive you crazy. My bicycle means a lot to me, it's like another part of my life. If someone wants to borrow it, I just say no, because it's like giving someone a newborn baby… You're scared they won't take care of it. Even when I'm sleeping and I hear something I just think of my bike. I can tell everyone who is thinking about getting a bicycle that it's a great idea, and that they shouldn't fuck with the taxis, man.'

Stephanie Baker
Pretorius Street, Arcadia, Pretoria, Gauteng, South Africa
2010/04/14 17:10

'I'm limited to cycling about one kilometre, in view of my age, and I use this bicycle, well, certainly every other day. I keep on the pavements, even though they're in a terrible state with chunks missing. Cycling is awfully good for public relations. I know the area's cleaners at the flats on my way to church – I get a greeting from them. The security men at the forensics place always wave, and you get to know people as you go along. Sometimes you see someone really looking quite gloomy and you give a bit of a smile and say *dumelang*, and get a smile back. I don't find this area hostile, I really don't. Some people living here are a bit frightened and, well, I don't think you can go about looking over your shoulder and expecting trouble. Most people have goodwill. If I didn't have the bicycle, I'd be more or less in retirement. At least I can get around and see the beauty of the place too. This bike suits me, it's quite old now and I'm 82 and three quarters. You know, I'm from England. When people see me, and I hear *haauw*, I think it is only mad dogs and Englishwomen who ride a bicycle, ha ha…'

Micky Abrahams
Corner Douglas Place and Victoria Road, Woodstock, Cape Town, Western Cape, South Africa
2010/04/07 18:05

'I ride around on this bike. I bought it there in Goodwood, from some people there, I think two years, no, three years ago. I bought it so I can just go on with life. I'm short of breath – with the bike I can go further. I ride my bike every day. I ride to Cape Town central, Sea Point and all around. And Goodwood and Tyger Valley. I live out on the road. On heaven's road. Out on the bushy ground, along the marsh where the rivers are. And places like that. I sleep out there at night. I hide my bike under the bushes when the thieves come around. Then they can't find it. When they see I've got no stuff they move on. I have these planks tied to the bike here – it's so I can pack stuff on top and tie it. Then I can at least get on with my life. You know, I love this bikey ... its name is Tractor-Tractor. I live on my own. In my own heaven. Down on the ground. Then I live here, then I live there, all over. For eight years already now I've been living all around. I like it like this. But I have to get some ground for me again, a home. I have to build up a home to go on further with my life. So life goes on...'

www.bicycleportraits.co.za

Graphic designer **Gabrielle Guy** and artist **Gabrielle Raaff** might share the same first name (which resulted in quite a few misdirected e-mails during the course of this project), but that's where the similarity between these two Capetonians ends. Gaby Guy loves making art books and taking afternoon naps. She currently owns a cheap '80s pink-and-white ladies' racer that she partly restored herself, although she hopes to upgrade to something cooler soon. Gabby Raaff (with an extra 'b') enjoys painting South African people and their neighbourhoods in watercolour from oblique angles, often using satellite imagery. Her bike was stolen a while ago and she is currently in the market for a well-travelled replacement.

This project would not have been possible without the support of Xander Smith, Hilton Tennant, Gary King, Brad Quartuccio, Guy Pearce, Henta and Dareen Engelbrecht, Nic and Sonia Grobler, Nora Swart, Roger and Elca Grobler, Olympic Cycles, Darrel Wratten, Johan Kotze, Henning Rasmuss, Louis de Waal, Simon Barlow, Christine Campbell, Ivin Greyling, Gordon Roy, Jean-Pierre Nortier, Joan Morgenstern, Mervyn Leong, Howard Pulchin, Owen Clipsham, Martin Palmer, Richard Bingham, Conrad Dempsey, Doug Ingram, Peter Newbury and Jörg Diekmann.

Published by Day One, 2012 / www.dayone.co.za / ISBN 978-0-620-52251-9

Design and layout Gabrielle Guy
Illustrations Gabrielle Raaff
Illustration assistance Allan and Jenny Raaff
Additional text Karen Robertson, Sean Wilson
Copy editing Deborah Louw, Ania Rokita
Translations Bolekwa Sesmani, Selloane Khalane, Atang Tshikare, Judy Brandao
Printing Tien Wah Press, Singapore

When **Stan Engelbrecht** and **Nic Grobler** initiated this project, they aimed for it to be a study of South African bicycle commuter culture. They wanted to find out who rides bicycles, why they ride them, if and why they love them, and of course why so few South Africans choose the bicycle as an alternative means of transport.

Stan's fascination with the mechanics of the bicycle and his background in photography, and Nic's interest in the role the bicycle plays in a community, brought them together to collaborate on a bicycle-related project. They imagined finding classic '70s Italian-built racers that had become hand-me-down commuter bikes, and photographing their weathered riders.

What started as a short ride around the area where they both live became a 6 000 kilometre journey over two years, taking them clear across the country. They traversed the Maluti mountains, sweated through Durban's humid climes, braved the blustery West Coast winds, got sunburnt outside Addo, and built up trashed bicycles in Maputo and rode them back to Johannesburg. They cycled everywhere to meet the bold individuals photographed for this project – people who choose to ride a bicycle in the face of cultural and social stigma, crime and dangerous roads.

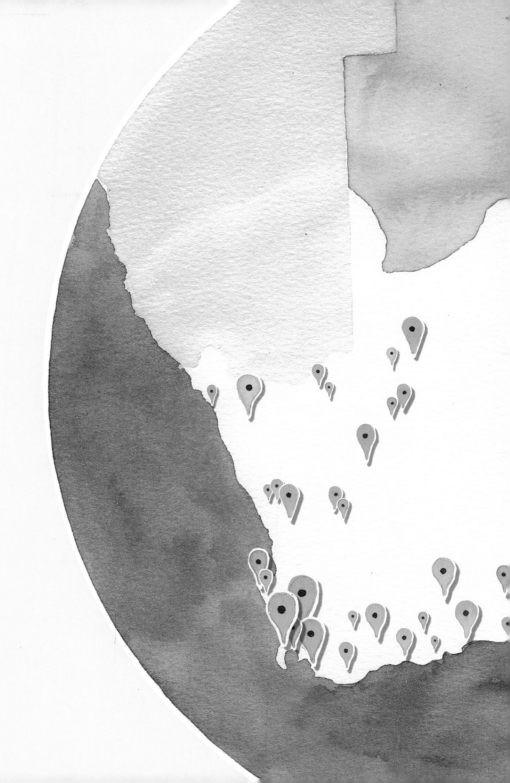